# Incarnation, Again

# Incarnation, Again

*Poems*

Elizabeth Harlan-Ferlo

RESOURCE *Publications* · Eugene, Oregon

INCARNATION, AGAIN
Poems

Resource Publications
An Imprint of Wipf and Stock Publishers
199 W. 8th Ave., Suite 3
Eugene, OR 97401

www.wipfandstock.com

PAPERBACK ISBN: 978-1-6667-3724-0
HARDCOVER ISBN: 978-1-6667-9649-0
EBOOK ISBN: 978-1-6667-9650-6

AUGUST 18, 2022 3:38 PM

"Don't Touch Me" contains two lines from "Visitation," from Sweet Machine by Mark Doty. Copyright (c) 1998 by Mark Doty. Used by permission of HarperCollins Publishers.

Cover art: *Pursed*, 2010. Sculpture by Linda Ekstrom. Courtesy of Pomona College Art Museum.

For my parents
*outward visible sign, inward spiritual grace*

Your whole Church, that wonderful and sacred mystery. . .

—Good Friday liturgy, *The Book of Common Prayer*

What the reader wants from reading and what the lover wants from love are experiences of a very similar design. It is a necessarily triangular design, and it embodies a reach for the unknown.

—Anne Carson, *Eros, The Bittersweet*

# Contents

*Acknowledgements* | *viii*

I

Get Close | 3
Mr. Right Theology | 6
Incarnation, Again | 7
Sunday, Varanasi/Manhattan | 9
Parish Acolyte | 11
A Reading: Can You See | 13
Judas Communion | 14
A Reading: Where You Go (Colombian Border Translation) | 15
Maundy Thursday Watch | 16
Subduction Zone Theology, Pentecost, 2011 | 17
Rectory | 18

II

*You Hate Nothing You Have Made* | 21
Sacrarium (Deepwater Horizon) | 22
Fig Season | 23
Cathedral, Granada | 24
Cathedral, Córdoba | 25
*Omnes Habitantes in Hoc Habitaculo* | 26
Red Sea, Amsterdam | 27
Rape Theology | 28
Fall, Rome | 29
A Reading: Many Times They Had Seized Him | 30
Judas at the Last Supper | 31
Rise to the Occasion | 32

III

A Reading: Your Faith Has Made You/Little Girl Get Up  |  37
Other Losses  |  39
Uterine Theology  |  40
Booty Call Theology  |  41
Don't Touch Me  |  42
Hapax Legomenon  |  43
Revised Lectionary  |  44
Exhalation  |  45

IV

Bible Study  |  49
Internet Comments Theology  |  50
From Whom All Blessings Flow  |  51
*Therefore Let Us Keep the Feast*  |  52
Advent  |  53
A Reading: Prepare  |  54
Divinity School  |  55
Church  |  57
Jesus Sandwich  |  59
Household Gods  |  60
A Reading: Be Opened  |  62
Narthex  |  63

*Notes*  |  65
*Gratitude*  |  67

# Acknowledgements

Grateful acknowledgement is made to the following publications in which these poems first appeared, some in different versions or with different titles.

*Anglican Theological Review*: "Exhalation"

*Bellingham Review*: "Rape Theology"

*Burnside Review*: "Get Close"

*Controlled Burn*: "A Reading: Prepare"

*Fourteen Hills*: "Don't Touch Me"

*Honey Pot, A Literary Miscellany*: "Revised Lectionary"

*LiturgicalCredo*: "Incarnation Again," "Sunday, Varanasi/Manhattan," and "Bible Study"

*Poet Lore*: "Fall, Rome"

*Psaltry & Lyre*: "Household Gods"

*Prick of the Spindle*: "*You Hate Nothing You Have Made*"

*Rock & Sling*: "Sacrarium"

*So to Speak*: "A Reading: Where You Go," "*Omnes Habitantes in Hoc Habitaculo*"

*Sugar House Review*: "Advent"

*The Sow's Ear Poetry Review*: "Red Sea, Amsterdam"

*Valparaiso Review*: "Uterine Theology"

*The Windhover*: "Parish Acolyte"

"Can You See" was written in response to a draft of, and then appeared in, *Sensing God: Reading Scripture with All Our Senses* from Cowley Publications.

"Bible Study" received Honorable Mention in the 2013 *Prick of the Spindle* Poetry Contest.

I

# Get Close

*Don't!—now you have to kiss it.*
Eve grabs my arm
as I slide the prayerbook

under my chair, its face
  to the synagogue rug.
I pick it up quick. An interfaith service.

        We are eight. Watching me watch her,
Eve puts her lips to the cover's
    (Hebrew/English)
        top edge.


                        ❀


        At our new parish
in New York City, men in tight T-shirts
worship the show:

    choir soaring behind the balustrade,
    brocaded clergy thronged with acolytes.

I think each single person a private loneliness.
Then, The Peace:
    faces and arms and mouths

            men offer each other,
                long-lost.


                        ❀

I find my father back in the sacristy,
hands a blush of black
        in a plastic bag of ashes, burst.

    He sees me, he sighs.
His clergy shirtfront brushed black again.
The table glitters. He

wedges the bag in the brass columbarium box,
    washes his hands at the sink that drains
        into the ground.

❀

            In college I swallow the Ganges,
a Varanasi temple.
The priest spoons it
    into my palm
    as blessing.

That morning, distant logs stacked dark as wounds
on the river's cremation ghat.

    The men who touch corpses can touch little else.
    Each hovers the shared cup over his lips.

❀

Every Sunday, they carry a book in,
    gilded. Lay it
gentle on the altar.

    *Mary startles at Gabriel*
        *Sita hears the rustling deer*
            *Isaac glints the knife*

In our front hall, the door's opened light
    glinting cellophane wrappers

marks the stacks
     as borrowed.

        ❀

     I hover behind a tour group,
near the petrified Cathedral-Mosque,
in a Córdoba synagogue's
shell.

     Their guide pauses his speech, then stops, waits. He speaks, repeats,
until up from the midst,
a plume of song

widens the walls,
     exhaling Hebrew back
in.

        ❀

     Two hours into the Good Friday service,
lines brim three aisles. We shuffle a crawl
toward a three-foot wooden cross,

pillow-propped,
blank without
corpus.

Every body leans in alone
     to stroke it,
     to kiss.

Gleam, varnish.
I touch with one finger, dead center.

# Mr. Right Theology

My dream men come

wearing bodies

and faces of other men.

Radhakrishnan proposed

true knowledge is not waking

life, but dreaming sleep, and higher

dreamless. Highest of all,

a knowing wholly other,

above those three. This morning,

Augustine surely disapproves

of my woman-mind,

my body grasping

*homoousion*, one

essence, Trinity.

I awake.

# Incarnation, Again

I see her first at the back of the church.
      I'll have to be nice to her
then she parades it in.

She of all people and Christmas morning

    dirty blonde hair and face amber light-filled
    from the hand-blown glass windows.

How dare she
a baby.


Last summer we all shepherded children:
tent to lake to washhouse to meals.
All of us were alike
in furtive trysts.

I'd resolved
to lose track
of virginity
the way you should a relative
    who won't
    stop

    drinking.
I spent womb-years
drugged with prevention,
    let the pills make me

    nothing. I told myself,
    in a minute, baby,
    not now,
    soon. I'm staring,

I'm trying
to look not at her I'm thinking

when Mary arrived
to visit
Elizabeth, it leaped up inside her,
        it knew. Liz burst out, sang.

The boyfriend arrives now, late,
half-proud.

    They were clearly
    fooling around; or she thought he
    was careful;
    or the condom broke.
    I'd settle for this
    regular miracle.

# Sunday, Varanasi/Manhattan

The sky before dawn mixes into the river,
merges to one world of smoke. Ganga
laps our boat of loose boards. She descends through
Shiva's topknot, tangled with ash and nits, so the world
won't drown. The sun's flat orange column makes horizon
to the women's splashing saris, to the brass pot the man
pours over his head, dips again. I lean over the broken
oarlock, set a banana leaf offering, lit, afloat.

❋

Sprawling newspaper pile on the kitchen table:
The *Magazine*, Week in Review, Sunday Styles.
My father and I scan the weddings for officiants he knows
and unlikely combinations. Ganga fills
a whole crinkly page in the *Magazine*.
A man's head emerges from ripples, holy lingam
gazing at us. A biologist. Each week,
he surrenders to Shiva's holy grime.

❋

Touring temples I leave my shoes outside
to cross mud-streaked floors. What we've brought
to the gods are ordinary things: thread, a sweets box
seeping grease. A priest sinks a dipper in the brass pot,
pours Ganga water into our palms, clear
against our skin. My friend, born in India,
puts her mouth to it so I do, imagining
my intestines coiling, the monkey's tail.

❋

Shiva rises a polished and faceless mound, lingam
blessed by a vertical stream. Water coats him,
slides into grooves in the circular base,
licking up petals and sandalwood paste. To win him,
Parvati sat for years in devotion. She had to

9

meditate enough to know she was a god.
The water trickles into an open-ended trough.
We touch just where it empties down.

❈

At Communion, for luck, I almost cross
my fingers below the shared cup. If God's in there
we can't get sick from the last person's mouth.
A biologist says washing our hands
poorly just moves germs around. After each sip,
the cup is wiped lipless, lipstick-less. Before touching
the Elements the Celebrant murmurs, *I wash my hands in innocence*
*and come to your altar, O Lord.*

# Parish Acolyte

### 1.

More than once, to keep from
playing with the white rope cincture,
twirling it, pulling the strings sticking out
like a Koosh ball from its knot, to keep from
watching people come to the rail, how they hold
their hands cupped for Communion,
I stare straight at the saints in adjoining panes
across the altar, high up on the facing wall.
Believe it or not I am good
at following instructions.
I count them over and over
in an endless-eyed tennis match,
hoping someone will notice.

### 2.

The woman who brings
apple pie every year on his birthday,
the Greek family who sends the triple-layer
chocolate tin every Christmas,
the parishioner who takes me to
*Phantom of the Opera*, to *Les Miserables*,
gives me hand-me-down sweaters;
the Search Committee man who demands
to "see his hands in the space";
the Search Committee woman who lets us stay
in her house while they clean the rectory,
the Search Committee man who, at the bar,
says, "You're a priest?" and a year later
stains the coffee table with overlapping wine rings;
the parishioner who lends us his cabin on the lake
and we stop up the septic;
the Impressionist who stops painting lucrative
sky-filled landscapes for Biblical scenes;

the intellectuals because he can preach,
the liturgy die-hards because he can sing,
the ones who send Christmas cards and leave off,
by accident, my mother's name;
the parish school-
boosters, all the priest-
wanna-bes, and the ones who leave
when he leaves, for good.

# A Reading: Can You See

Mark 8:22–25

It was a long walk out of the village. So he asked
Jesus, whose hand in his was sweaty, what things looked
        like.   Jesus told him
   wheel tracks creased the road,
   the sky stretched, washed out,
   sandal straps echoed on his skin.

When Jesus had put saliva on his eyes,
laid his hands on, he asked him,   Can you see
        anything?
   Asked by his mother,
   by boys throwing rocks,
   by his own tongue in the dark.

The man looked.
There are

      people, they look like trees
       walking. Their   eyes and   mouths,

olives, to be picked,
their fingers shake
like leaves.
   The trees are walking,   their roots
       breathe   dust.

   Jesus touched his eyes again.

# Judas Communion

John 13:21–30

I'll show you where she hid when the cops came,
her twin sister tells me, touching

the sliding closet door. From a high window,
ground-level sunlight angles over

a neatly-made bed that takes up
the whole room. We go back up into

the summer between seventh and eighth grade.
The police are going to release the man

her twin sister calls her boyfriend.
We walk back to their house, near school,

where the thin branch broke and she fell
the night she snuck out to meet him.

It was after that night I told my father
what they were doing. I went to his office

to tell him, and he made a call.
Yet only last year, and all the years before,

every Wednesday at Eucharist before
the potluck, the twins came into

the Lady Chapel for Communion,
then dashed out early, pounding down the hallway

outside the door. But I had to wait,
with all the adults, for the Blessing.

# A Reading: Where You Go
# (Colombian Border Translation)

Ruth 1:14–18

They came for her father but he wasn't there
so they reached for the daughter, María José.
The mother said to the men from the jungle,

> *si llevan a la niña me llevan a mí.*
> Do not press me to leave you
> or to turn back from following.

Perhaps, she later told the reporter,
to avoid getting into a loud shouting match,
he kidnapped us both.

# Maundy Thursday Watch

A wake for anticipation. Awake: the goal. A waiting

    Newsprint board in the parish hall limned with time slots. At midnight,
    my father crosses the rectory driveway,

    and again at four am, if no one signs up for then.
    The church is stripped, wood-bared, sheened in the dim.

There are hours for which to atone. Someone must wake up for them

    My father sits. Tomorrow: a long service, what's still
    undone? Done and left undone

    the Altar of Repose blooms
    the wafer box

# Subduction Zone Theology, Pentecost, 2011

Acts 2:1–4
Matthew 27:51


Altar bristles lupine's pink tentacles, red hot poker's
yellow-red staves. Smokebush branches huff sticky, purple breath.

Rivers are running unseasonably high. American exegesis:
any place can catch fire. On the tongues of Christchurch, of Tōhoku,

the Temple curtain still hangs, tattered. My bluff overlooks
Willamette flats: train cars, trucks, and cranes will drown first,

Union Pacific smokestack will gasp like a fish,
crumble into the fullness of time. No warning, no sign.

# Rectory

I am up late studying when she calls, the renter above the parish office
where someone's walking around downstairs, she wants to see if maybe
my father is working late she says someone is definitely there and maybe
she should call the police I say yes definitely call the police I say because
he is here asleep. I hang up I know if I get him he will go over now, put on
clothes and fumble for keys in the dark. I picture someone sifting through
the church offices. I picture them faceless and hulking. With guns or a
knife. The street edges glow orange, the center white line broken green,
green, then yellow then red still red still red the cabs idling through their
teeth as each drawer opens I should wake him I will not wake him yet.

II

## You Hate Nothing You Have Made

We come in from rain for Lent's beginning,
first of many solemn days. In the windowless,
wood-walled church, we're in mid-mutter when the ashes float
   up from their small glass bowl. They spiral,
   cascade the altar in billowing snakes. They split, prismatic
      shimmering colors slithering across the floor.
      Red ash climbs my legs, winds my feet,
         swirls turquoise to my waist. It sticks. It
            sticks, it sticks. The priest stares at his purpling hands,
            a woman scrapes her blinding blue throat, a man grabs
               his chartreuse belly. Another drops to his knees, ochre
                  spreading from thighs. Ash swoops, rising, splotching us
                     umber, viscous magenta. Ash chokes
                     open mouths as out of our bodies
                        the room fluoresces . . .

# Sacrarium (Deepwater Horizon)

Soil where the pipe cuts off     saturates
with the leavings    of that which is blessed.
    Crumbs brushed from hands.
    Dumped bowl of ashes.
    What falls from shaken altar cloth.
    The rinse water following.

Anything consecrated gotten rid of
must drain here,
into earth: terminus.    Except we know better
   of bones and skin. How they reduce,    die into
what lives. How towering ex-holies get razed,
   crumble, then layer, compress

to underwater plumes'
flayed chemical beauty,
   black and shining gushing
   tongues:
     death of resurrection.
     Drunk on the residue.
Our hands orange-stained from dragging the boom.

# Fig Season

Mark 11:13

Tell ripeness by feel, she laughs,
cupping each testicle-weight
in her palm. The tree is heavy summer afternoon
as we squint up into it, out in her garden.
Weeks now, since he was born; years
they'd had to try, to yield.
The baby boy is inside,
with his father.

❀

Last week, lunch with a mother
who woke to a disappointed
surgeon, a woman who found
nothing (no cysts, no fibroids,
no egg at all)
under the leaf of her skin.
This last was the last
of the ones they'd saved.
No one knows, she said, why I
eat embryos. Her mouth laughs.

❀

High up in the tree, out of reach,
bees gather to suck one open. How much
time will the tree have before it
withers? Green fruit fills up
the bag I hold. The father
brings him out now laughing into
view. I can barely hide
my naked desire,
what I would take
if it grew.

# Cathedral, Granada

They built it the usual way:
  where the mosque
  was standing.

Outside, there are no fountains
  for ablutions, no place for
  rows of dusty shoes.

Instead, beggars linger on the steps, thrust
  rosemary cuttings,
  offering to bless us,

purify our pockets.
  Dirt caked deeply
  under their fingernails.

Christians in their early days
  were avoided at all costs:
  they claimed you need only

one bath in your life.
  My friends don't know not
  to smile. I hustle by,

dodge through the door—if you touch
  what's offered,
  they'll never leave you alone.

# Cathedral, Córdoba

Frozen holy
   violence gone
delirious under the skin:


red and white arches, palm fronds
   of the mosque oasis, seed
intruder Gethsemane.


An idol-scrawled reredos
   glows amid trees.
Benediction shadows hang


like vines. Bespeckled, blind,
   the *mihrab* hunches, strains
silence for the ninety-nine names.


Floors buckle eastward
   under Sunday processions, writhing
for prayer mats, foreheads, shins.


Inside its glass walls, the Eucharist thrusts
   monstrance spines
toward the pillared trees, *banderillas*


to stab the back,
   to prolong
a spectacular death.

## Omnes Habitantes in Hoc Habitaculo

Ode on chasuble in New Spain

(*Friar*) I cut the boning out, the missing body,
   slid through slits to let the dress
   binding fall. I cut off
   her sleeves. They call it *poncho* here.
   I, *chasuble*, my "little house."

   (*Doña*) I send the dress into nothingness; the world drops off
     at the edge. Still, we all eat this God,
     each wife to gone-*hidalgo*.

(*Friar*) I dream I am naked, roofless.
   My hands, rough, catch. I pray
   for the fall of mankind—my *sursum corda*
   hems every sanctified in with the cursed.
   How, O Lord, do I map this place?

   (*Doña*) At night, his body burns against ghost-skin
     inside my dress made man. I move
     *per ipsum et cum ipso et in ipso.*

(*Friar*) My hands touch silk—Castilla, *mea maxima culpa,*
   this embroidered morning, bud by bud,
   I labor to build your shape. Maria, your dress
   new-worldly stained, transfigured,
   Maria, your whiteness to clay.

   (*Doña*) Priest, swing open the door and raise
     up your womb of blood and bread.
     Sew my Christ with mud and gold.

# Red Sea, Amsterdam

Jammed sidewalks, adrift
in drunk and clamoring pink-faced men.
Two couples, we clutch hands, course

single-file. Men spill off the curbs
into streets lined with doors of glass.
They jostle and shout, stare in:

a woman in a bra, curls kinky; a woman
with blonde-streaked gray; a woman, short,
black-bobbed, bored. Each perches, inches

from us. Three hours before,
I'd walked here, I'd passed a woman
pushing her stroller down these

then-shuttered streets, grocery bags
balanced, both handles. Canals stretch out
dark tongues as we weave through

men forming walls on the left
and right, pressing in, bodies
bathed in each door's neon stripe.

# Rape Theology

Lake Garda's beach is pavement slab.
I wade through skin-litter to find my spot.
Swans smooth across the green water,
their necks soft snakes, curved columns.

A feather slip-skims the shallows
as I step into the opaque. One swan
slides closer, water shifting the thought
of claws. My skin ripples, already crouched

in knee-deep shallows, my bottom half
sunk in gray. He narrows the water between us
and I remember they mate for life, once
they've chosen. The one whose body

Zeus borrowed went searching
for Leda. He found reeds crushed,
her flattened swipe-shape. After that,
who of his own would have him?

The black-edged eyes do not ignore me.
I blink across the water's thin smell
and throw back my shoulders, go still.
There's no way to know who's god.

# Fall, Rome

My father keeps September shuttered out of the bedroom
in the rental apartment in Rome. My father can't
get up because the towers have fallen
on either side of his spine. People covered in dust
are walking north in Lower Manhattan,
past his parish.
He's not there.
My mother and I angle our legs over his,
piling up layers of cloth and skin, balancing
between the double bed's twin moats. We coax.
Outside, the gleaming piazzas burn with news,
full of more people he might betray. He was
at Hadrian's theater, its inaccessible island,
an architectural illusion. He'd been sliding
the cloudless blue over the lens of his camera
while people are stumbling from Lower Manhattan,
covered in ash, to his parish. He can't go
anywhere now. Noon presses the windows. I offer
a *Kindersorpresa* egg, a rattling hollow of foil.
We scatter the chocolate shell over our tongues.
Dad pries open the plastic yolk, then waves off
the toy, its minuscule directions. My mother takes
the pieces and assembles, snaps wheels
on a tiny car. We sit while he rolls it over
the pile of our arms and legs.

# A Reading: Many Times They Had Seized Him

Luke 8:26–39

Please        send us—      (not the abyss)

  we are no earth    we are no breath-earth    only breath

steaming      the lake's surface    above the bloated swine—


the man, even chained    (something to break    against the skin)

  even sleeping in tombs    (another skin    sloughed)

send us back    into—look    how

  they fear him    more    without us

# Judas at the Last Supper

His mouth closes on each fried hand-pie
while the crowd keeps count against the record
posted on the cart's sliding window. He chews,
crouched, swathed in the roaring
heat lamp of the parking lot's asphalt corner,
hunched at the picnic table's slats. He hollows
as the crowd hoots, calling his name. He'll
consume them in thirty, make them free.
A camera lens shoves closer. He pants, gasps,
eyes flat in the light reflected by puddles,
by the glass of water at his elbow,
by the trash can's black plastic maw.

# Rise to the Occasion

Sit a few rows from the front on the left, not right near the pulpit where we're under his nose.

Stand up when we stand up together. Cross your hands over your chest if you don't want it. Go back down the center aisle.

Here, some crayons.

Yes, you have to stay for the last hymn. Sing unison on the final verse, that's for the organ to play something extra.

Come say hello to the bishop.

No, don't wait for your father we'll see him later; don't forget to eat a bagel before you come over.

That dress doesn't look quite right for church.

Quiet when you come in late. That skirt is awful short for church. If nobody goes up, just go up anyway. Go back by the side aisle, not the center.

No, your father has a meeting.

That blouse is see-through. Be polite to Mrs. P—when she invites you, please write a thank you note.

No, your father has a meeting.

You don't have to come but it would be nice if you were there. Yes you have to stay the whole time if you come.

Come say hello to the bishop.

Don't leave your shoes in the front hall there will be 75 people here after. No, your father has a meeting.

If you come down, be presentable.

Come down when you're ready.

# III

# A Reading: Your Faith Has Made You/Little Girl Get Up

Mark 5:21–43

I scramble back
up from the ditch, the rising dust,
where the men elbow-pushed me
out of the crowd.

My mother: have you not had enough of their cures, of their hands?
My sister said, Go. The way
others do when they see.

Pain slides out wet.
Pain stays, roils.
A grunt-breath, the belly clenches.
(He'd calmed the storm in the boat.)

As the crowd moves they move me, eyes closed.
A face arrives:
a girl who lies
too still.

I open them then, I push
past a man, past another.
I can see his back, his robe.
He sees that girl? He sees—

Blood running the inside of my thigh, rolling to the ankle.
I reach between men's bodies, I try to reach and someone sees
blood on my dress,
shouts, kicks out my feet

I pitch forward, I grab

  to keep from falling—
—the girl

# Other Losses

Two hundred forty lines he knocks out Eve
—some thirty pages—Milton's angel then
shows Adam future-earth's grand glory, death.
But ear to ground, Eve finds she's clay again,
unraveled body, mixed in dust. The dirt
vibrates with voices pitched like hers, alive
and chanting names. *Innana! Isis!* howl
the crowd of witnesses. And then a call,
response sung back. *According to your word.*
The sounds course through her, stitching light until
she wakes. She feels her lining hum. Far off,
sideways, man and angel. She sits up then,
against the ground, opens her legs, her lips:
first offering, post-paradise, first blood.

# Uterine Theology

Crocuses lesion winter purple, expose
snow's incurable ground.

Brusque highway: rough on its edges.

Geese-line beneath clouds: iron filings,
a fourth row of black placebos,
hardened appointments.

Heedless of borrow ponds, a few drift
onto the median.          Fat ashes, so intent,

they build nests between the lanes.

# Booty Call Theology

I'm not ashamed, I tell myself, to claim
it. Yet I use Episcopal, not the name
Christian. That's for those others, tin-
eared, ignorant, whose faith begins
and remains in judgment. Not the same

as mine. I was born first to ritual, came
even in utero to the Word. They aimed,
my folks, for literary redemption.
    I am not ashamed.

College weekend nights, a regular game.
Each Saturday liturgy the same:
flexed calves and hips, Christian's
skin presses into mine. Joy and chagrin
on the dark walk home: incarnate claim.
    I am not ashamed.

# Don't Touch Me

John 20:11–17

**1.**

What I screamed at her—mother—
meaning the opposite. Honed
to cut both ways.

**2.**

Withdrawal: I will lay you
out sweating on the ER gurney.
I'm addicted to what I'm selling.

**3.**

Jesus to Mary: Things are different now.
What you would want if you came back.
With less body.

**4.**

I can't sleep with you anymore I said, not until you know.
What you want, not what you want wounded.
And what shows the wound.

**5.**

Protection, it's also protection's opposite.
Jesus to Mary: *What did you think,*
*that joy was some slight thing?*

# Hapax Legomenon

In a tiny book she made, my mother
listed every verb in the poems

I wrote, even auxiliaries, even
infinitives. Each folio held

another: minute doorways
opening out and out and out.

In her studio, she confirms the fold's
attempt to subvert distance,

bone folder warming each page
to half, to double, in her hands. We are

each other's singular occurrence.
The night I arrive we stay up too late,

filling distance with words. When she made
that book I was writing how people try

to speak when explanation
feels impossible. After we touch all

the new things she's made, my mother
restacks her makeshift press—thick dictionaries,

her green Plato penciled with Greek glosses
—to weigh each word closed.

There were so many, she said,
so few repeats.

## Revised Lectionary

I want to know what you said. Not to
the visitor—we have that—but after,
   to Joseph, one,
     then the rest of the town. Because

the calendar tells that you bear
this again,
again. First Priest, tell me,

what do you say? Listen,
my great-grandmother Jennie made seven,
her daughter, eight. With what phrases—

(curved kingdomscape in the gullet)—do you
write the Word?
   They tell it now

   as if we are bodies, empty,
   tombs.

# Exhalation

At evening, a young Banyarwanda woman
places a clay pot of water at the door.
It's not for beggars or animals
full of night-thirst. God will use
the water to make a child.

We start as fish, by floating.
Later our tail and gills dissolve,
fins split into fingers. Transparent
water makes earth-colored skin.
Water, not bread, becomes flesh.

Early morning wafts
across the doorway,
wrinkles the skin
of a reflected sky.

IV

# Bible Study

I see it fall open, quick-scan the whole week—
   rectangles scribbled with names and times:
     his tiny black book I am never to look in—
       as the garage rattles shut under

me and my mother. He'd tossed it on the counter,
   his keys and his collar skittering away
     after the drive from a back booth
       where he goes every Tuesday with three other

priests. Bar smoke
   wafts from his suede bomber jacket
     and thin black shirt,
       from the book kept in his breast pocket,

its gold-cross-stamped cover now pressed open flat.
   On today: *BS* (a scrawled smudge.)
     I point: what's this? And he reaches past me
       to close it, eyes widening, mouth pursed

in delight. Bible Study, he says,
   giving the book a push down the counter.
     It slides into the collar's
       white curve of blunt teeth.

# Internet Comments Theology

Matthew 7:3–5

First a side branch, then another, higher,
swish-falls. A faceless figure balanced
eye level, lifts the growling saw—a third branch

drops, sapling weight. I stiffen
for a noisy beheading but the face mask lifts
and a man wipes his eyes with his sleeve,

wipes again. Grinding woke me:
full-empty gnashing of branches
undercut, then forced into the chipper.

I think the man has something
in his eye. I watch from my window.
He stands on what he's cutting down.

# From Whom All Blessings Flow

The paper cup's metal rattle of the man
on the way-home corner of Grove and Bleecker:
Down payment on my yacht?   Shake jingle
   white-lipped mouth for heavy nickels, scrap-dime slivers.

During the offertory hymn, my mother tries to tear her check
   from the checkbook quietly and thus
   slow-ly,
   slow-ly, tiny rip, rips:
the weekly pledge I get to drop
in the gilt and velvet plate. (Once I said why bother

  we just get it back in Dad's salary and—
    first of all because that's not how it works
    but second of all because
I was, in a way, right
    we pledge just like everyone else.)

## Therefore Let Us Keep the Feast

My grandmother sets the bowl
full on the table. "There's fruit,"

she says. "Do you want some fruit?"
No, we have sat eating dinner for hours.

She offers each. "Do you want
a plum? There's grapes. Have some grapes."

We are fine, no, no, we are full.


At two a.m., the dishwasher
hisses to stillness. After the last,

last game of cards, each body gone up
the stairs in the dark, the lamp of stained-glass

pears and apples haloes the table.
She wipes down the plastic tablecloth,

raises up the near-empty bowl.

## Advent

The wind shifts even the sound
of the train pulling out. Shrill stop's ending

begins its impetus, leans
   into move. The wind
knows to move:

in front of the house,
purple leaves shuffle from a neighbor's tree;
crisp flutters, like fried beet shavings,
skim over the sidewalk.

Inside, the animals
   push into any space
my half-folded body makes.
The leaves pulled down,

now not enough. Three blocks the wind brings
the sound, through a closed window;
   the wind vaults
   its coax of the train:
come on now, it's time,
come now, c'mon.

# A Reading: Prepare

Matthew 3:1–6

It's the smell that first arrives
then the sky buzzing. The man's
      skin clings
         taut as a fishing net.

Bent elbow, bent wrist,
    fingers curled and split, he beckons, hands
  dripping river.

Your sweat slips
    down edges of skin,
        seeps through your toes    and you think,

I'll creep in,
even though
you remember before, how

      you found
      yourself under,

the sky of your lungs    torn open.

# Divinity School

We were leaving by ship towards map-lands:
  Kenya,
  India,
  China,
  malaria—I was twelve, couldn't
swallow chalky *Lariam:*
thick disks, and bitter.
My mother charted a length of blue cardboard,
glued on twenty bits, each bigger
than the last, for practice:
  *Colored sprinkle,*
  *sesame seed,*
  *rice grain,*
  *lentil,*
and I paced between sink and gaping tub;
deep breaths, big water gulps,
  *lentil,*
  *kernel,*
  *Red-Hot,*
  *raisin,*
coughs. I touched them like a statue's
outstretched foot, blessing-smoothed;
  *raisin,*
  *Tic-Tac,*
  *M&M,*
  *vitamin.*
The edges wrinkled from sink-splash
like the blue laugh of Baby Krishna, who loves
to steal butterballs. His mother
peers into his throat:

*Masai Mara*
*sunrise,*
*Kanchipuram*
*temple lotus,*
*Li River*
*gumdrop mountain.*

# Church

**1.**

Chapel of the Bedroom on-the-Airshaft, Chapel of the Elevator Tantrums, Chapel of the Roaches-in-the-Walls, Chapel of the Refectory Beans, Chapel of the Saturday Jaunt, Chapel of the Bathroom Haircuts

**2.**

Church of St. Scaffolding, Church of St. Liturgy in-the-Gym, Church of St. Bus-Pass-Taped Lunchbox, Church of St. Pink-Rug Nap-Time, Church of St. Frank's Deli Ham and Mayo

**3.**

Church of the Mountain of Grits, Church of the Missed Kindergarten Graduation in White Dresses, Church of the Pollen on-the-Blacktop, Church of the Spelling Test Half-Sheet, Church of the Stuffed Animal Blessing, Church of the Rotting Playhouse in-the-Backyard

**4.**

Church of Slate-Roof Rectory, Church of Caked-Foundation Ladies, Church of Third Pew from the Front, Church of Meetings Meetings Meetings, Church of JCC After-School & Late-Pick-up Shabbat, Church of Folding Chairs on Linoleum, Church of Pizza and Cake, Church of Youth Group Songbooks, Church of Parish Secretary Perfume On-the-Receiver, Church of Bishop Demanding Altar Calls, Church of Gay AA

**5.**

Sabbatical Cathedral-at-Sea, St. Protest Sculpture Cathedral, All Colonial Hymns Cathedral, St. One-Hundred-Year-Old-Egg Cathedral

**6.**

Church of St. Whole City Block, Church of St. Snackless Coffee Hour, Church of St. Incense Pot Around-The-World, Church of St. Basement Thrift Shop, Church of St. Paid Choir, Church of St. Ten-Page Easter Vigil Instructions, Church of St. Dinner with the Presiding Bishop, Church of St. Just Take a Cab, Church of St. Are We Rich, Church of St. Private

Garden, Church of St. Pride Parade, Church of St. Bishop Elections, Church of St. Boyfriends, Church of St. Cast Parties, Church of St. College Decision Envelopes

7.

Hook-Up Church, Heard of Your Father Church, Smarmy Sermons Cathedral, Barefoot You Can Feel It Better Memorial Church, Chapel of St. Paycheck, Church of the Broken Mic, Church of St. Praise Choir & Bilingual Good Friday, Church of St. Mattress on the Springs, Wildwood Trail Church, Church of St. Saturday Night Salsa, Church of St. Once in A While, Church of the Made it At Least Before-the-Gospel, Church of Third Pew from the Back

# Jesus Sandwich

I was five, I practiced first
in the sacristy, in seminary
My mother says, maybe
it turns to God
inside you
Take this

to the piscina, or outside
for the birds
My father says
the Mass his Catholic mother requests

in her living room newly ordained
card table set up by the fireplace
unsteady legs on the rug
the summoned Uncles watch

a whole loaf from the family bakery
My father consecrates
all of it
He says
take this
Uncle Vinnie, here's
enough to last you till next time

# Household Gods

*Cicero, De Domo Sua*

Jesus hangs golden in my grandmother's house
on polished cherrywood in each bedroom.
Two palm branches, slightly slipped from their x,
press between cross and wall.

*The most sacred,*
*the most hallowed place on earth:*

Outside, snow cracks sidewalks
and factory windows. My grandfather
digs out the car, drives the empty streets of Rome, New York,
to his cousin's bakery, to deliver the bread.

*the home*
*of each and every citizen.*

In the kitchen, a plaque proclaims Him
unseen guest at every meal.

❋

Jesus ascends in my father's house
between the front windows,
an Impressionist white smudge with hands.
He rides the dark while two figures below look up.

*There are his sacred hearth*
*and his household gods,*

Outside, yellow cabs and delivery trucks
thump over the perpetual steel plate in the street.
My mother, returning, sets them down:
two bags, one full of books.

*the very center*
*of his worship.*

On the way to the kitchen, stained glass panel, lit:
"In the Beginning was the Word."

# A Reading: Be Opened

Mark 7:31–35

They crouched against the wall, away
from the crowd. Air-smell: shore and sweat.
The deaf man ground his teeth, scuffed, finally

poked him, then touched his own: Ears!
   (Touch!   Touch, touch.)   Jesus looked,
   grabbed—drove the fingers
in.

The deaf man jerked them out,
heaved to clench
fists.

But Jesus spat in his own hands,
cupped the deaf man's jaw, reached in, touched
quick the tongue. The man snapped to bite,
swallowed:

   salt, dust, the memory of bread.

   Then
water broke loose, roared.
   Christ's lips moved    like a stone,
                rolling away. The man unfurled
                his hands
                his mouth.

# Narthex

This is almost the church and not yet quite the church.
Sometimes eddies the overflow, holiday tides.
It's threshold, not gutter.

   Every week, toes on a boundary renegotiating:
   edge slow or get soaked?
      The Rabbis said, the miracle is not the sea parted,
      but that the people walked in.

Scythe, decisive—
skitter-slip constant strokes.
Through waist-high air,
make openings
   seamless expectation (Prelude ends)
   that close just as smoothly behind (procession people crowd)

—the service begins.

# Notes

"Mr. Right Theology." Hindu philosopher Sarvepalli Radhakrishnan (1888-1975) argued that the highest level of knowledge was actually three steps beyond our conscious perception. The doctrine codified at the Council of Nicea was of the Creator and Son as one essence (homoousion.) Later the Holy Spirit was added. Augustine elaborated on this doctrine. He also had a lot of things to say about women.

"A Reading: Where You Go (Colombian Border Translation)." The quoted fourth line, roughly translated, means, 'If you're taking the girl, you're taking me too.' Much of the poem is taken directly from the report, "Colombian guerrillas cross into Venezuela looking for new hostages for ransom" which aired on "The World" from Public Radio International.

"*Omnes Habitantes in Hoc Habitaculo.*" Aristocratic Spanish wives donated their out-of-fashion gowns to friars in the so-called New World to use for chasubles. This poem was inspired by a fourteenth-century chasuble on exhibit at the Yale University Art Gallery and imagines a conversation between two such people about this garment. The title and phrases in the third, fourth, and fifth stanzas come from the Latin Missal. The title means 'all those who dwell in this house.' A key phrase of Eucharistic consecration is in the fourth stanza: "through him and with him and in him."

"Other Losses" references a moment in Book XI of *Paradise Lost*.

"Don't Touch Me." The final lines are from Mark Doty's beautiful poem, "Visitation," published in *Sweet Machine*.

"Hapax Legomenon" means a singular occurrence of a word in a body of work.

"A Reading: Prepare" was inspired by an ink sketch by Mike Van, Church of the Resurrection service leaflet, Eugene, Oregon, 2003.

"Divinity School" references the tenth canto of the Bhagavata Purana.

"Church" is offered in memory of The Rev. Jonathan Glass.

"Household Gods." The painting is by Simon Carr.

# Gratitude

These poems were fed by the high level of scholarship and mentoring in the Oberlin College Religion Department, especially by Dr. Paula Richman. Thanks also to the University of Oregon Humanities Center and to the Port Townsend Writing Conference at Centrum, both of which assisted by providing space, resources, and community encouragement. I am grateful for a residency at the Vermont Studio Center with the June 2015 Barbara White Studios crew, especially Sara Mumolo and DeMisty Bellinger. Thanks to Rusty Morrison for her generous feedback at the Colrain Conference.

Thank you to The Episcopal Church and its parishes. I think.

Much appreciation to the teachers who guided the creation of some of these poems in their earliest stages, in particular, Martha Collins, David Young, Pimone Triplett, and Dorianne Laux. Thanks also to the Poem-A-Day teams, especially Walt Schaefer and Lisa Oliver.

Wayne Bund, Rick Rees, Robin Schauffler, Catherine Bull, Rajiv Mohabir, and Laura Passin gave feedback on this manuscript at critical points, and I value their wisdom, literary and otherwise. Thank you to Richa Dasgupta, who took me to the Ganges, and to Cheryl Harlan, who welcomed me to the Salish Sea.

Thank you to Wyn Cooper for painstaking and cheerful editing, and encouragement. Any theological, grammatical, or literary errors that remain are my own. Deep gratitude to Linda Ekstrom for the use of the altered Bible on the cover, and for her work with feminism and biblical texts.

Thank you to Nathan LaRud for being a great preacher as well as a friend and one-man clearness committee. Thank you, Linda Z., for the teachings and the company. Thank you to my parents for your unshakable loyalty, exuberance, and faith.

Thank you, Matt, for slowing me down and building me up. I am grateful for you every day. Finally, *baci baci* to two chambers of my heart: Annie and Raffa.